COLOR

FROM RAINBOWS TO LASERS

COLOR

FROM RAINBOWS TO LASERS

Franklyn M. Branley

Illustrated by Henry Roth

Thomas Y. Crowell Company · New York

Copyright © 1978 by Franklyn M. Branley
Illustrations copyright © 1978 by Henry Roth
All rights reserved. Except for use in a review,
the reproduction or utilization of this work in
any form or by any electronic, mechanical, or
other means, now known or hereafter invented,
including xerography, photocopying, and record-
ing, and in any information storage and retrieval
system is forbidden without the written permission
of the publisher. Published simultaneously in
Canada by Fitzhenry & Whiteside Limited, Toronto.
Manufactured in the United States of America

Library of Congress Cataloging in Publication Data
Branley, Franklyn Mansfield
Color, from rainbows to lasers.
Bibliography: p. Includes index.
SUMMARY: Explains the basic composition of color,
how it is created and used, and its psychological
effects.
1. Color—Juv. lit. [1. Color]
I. Roth, Henry. II. Title.
QC495.5.B7   535'.6   76-46304
ISBN 0-690-01256-X
0-690-03847-X(LB)

10 9 8 7 6 5 4

Contents

By Franklyn M. Branley

Comets, Meteoroids, and Asteroids:
   Mavericks of the Solar System

The Earth: Planet Number Three

Energy for the 21st Century

Experiments in Sky Watching

Experiments in the Principles of Space Travel

Lodestar: Rocket Ship to Mars

Man in Space to the Moon

Mars: Planet Number Four

The Milky Way: Galaxy Number One

The Moon: Earth's Natural Satellite

The Nine Planets

Pieces of Another World:
   The Story of Moon Rocks

Solar Energy

The Sun: Star Number One

COLOR

FROM RAINBOWS TO LASERS

Light Waves and Light Energy

What is color? Why should a pencil appear to be yellow rather than red? Why does the color of the sky vary from gray to blue to red, orange, or green? Why is a rose red while a morning glory is blue? For more than two thousand years, as far back as Aristotle—and probably much further—men have been seeking answers to such questions. We shall explore, among other aspects of color, the answers that have been offered down through the centuries. We'll discover, as often is the case, that many of the guesses made by early investigators were proved to be correct through experiments devised to test their theories.

Without light there would be no color. Therefore, to understand color one must have some understanding of what light is, how it is produced, how it travels from place to place.

Early Greek philosophers believed that light was composed of some kind of particles. Objects threw off these particles. In some fashion they traveled through the space between the object and the viewer. The particles passed into a person's eye, where, in some unknown way, an image of the object was produced.

Other Greek scholars, Aristotle among them, disagreed with the particle theory. They believed that light resulted from some kind of action (just what kind was never explained) that occurred between the object and the viewer. The space separating the two was transparent, so the "action" itself could be observed.

Neither of these explanations was adequate. Actually they revealed very little; still, they were the basis of the "science of light" until the early part of the seventeenth century. In the 1630s René Descartes (1596–1650), a famous French philosopher, mathematician, and scientist, proposed a new theory to explain light. Essentially it was a combination of the earlier particle idea and the action idea. Descartes said that light traveled from one place to another by pressure (or action), from whatever produced the light, through the particles that lay between, and thus to the eye.

Descartes compared light and seeing to the way in which a blind man finds his way with a stick or cane. When his cane encounters stones, sidewalk, water, or soft earth, the blind man knows the difference by the different pressures that are sent along the stick. The pressures are felt by his hand and the information is sent to his brain, where it is interpreted. In a similar way, Descartes said, no particles traveled from an object into a person's eye; there was only a pressure on the particles that filled up the space between the object and one's eye. The rays of light that are occasionally revealed, as when there is dust in the air, were the lines along which these pressures were sent.

This idea of Descartes's—that light is pressure moving through the particles in space—stimulated the thinking of other investigators. One of these was Christian Huygens (1629–1695), a Dutch scientist who first suggested the wave theory of light. At his time it was known that a wave in water starts at a given point and travels along the surface. Also, it was known that sound travels through air. Huygens carried the idea one step further.

Light, he said, was a wave that traveled from "ether molecule to ether molecule." Ether was considered to be a substance that filled all space. For more than two hundred years people believed in the "ether." Less than one hundred years ago it was still used to explain how light travels. Toward the end of the past century, however, an experiment proved there is no such substance.

Although "ether" was nonexistent, other aspects of Huygens' theory of light were essentially correct, as was found out later. However, at the time the theory was proposed, it was not accepted. The main reason for its lack of success was the fact that the great Sir Isaac Newton did not believe in it.

At that time Isaac Newton (1642–1727) was considered by many to be the most outstanding of all scientists, philosophers, and mathematicians. So great was his popularity that whatever he proposed was immediately accepted. Newton held that light was made of corpuscles, or particles. His followers believed this meant that Newton discounted the wave nature of light entirely. Therefore, according to Newton (or so his followers believed), light was particles thrown out by a light source. The particles traveled through space and entered the eye, just as many of the early Greeks had said. Because of Newton's support, the corpuscular, or particle, theory of light dominated thinking for another hundred years.

But there were skeptics. Investigation showed that light would go right through a vacuum. How could that be if light was made of particles? Also, light went through glass and water without disturbing them at all. Many people believed that light occurred instantaneously.

But the Danish astronomer Ole Roemer (1644–1710) proved otherwise. He measured the time intervals between eclipses of the satellites of Jupiter. When Earth was close to Jupiter, the eclipses occurred at the predicted times. But as Earth moved away from Jupiter, the eclipses occurred later and later. At the greatest distance the time difference was about 1000 seconds.

Roemer said that was because the light from the satellite took 1000 seconds to travel the diameter of Earth's orbit. (This was known to be about 186,000,000 miles.) Roemer said that light could not occur spontaneously since it took time for it to travel from one place to another. Light traveled very fast. When distances were short, light seemed to occur all at once; but when distances were great, the travel time could be measured. Light took 1000 seconds to travel 186,000,000 miles, he said, so the speed of light was 186,000 miles per second:

$$\text{Speed of light} = \frac{186,000,000}{1000} = 186,000 \text{ mps}$$

Actually, because the diameter of Earth's orbit was not known exactly, and because of errors in measurement, Roemer's result was somewhat less than this. However, his procedure was correct. And later experiments verified that the speed of light is close to 186,000 miles per second. In the metric system the speed of light is usually given as 3×10^{10}—read "three times ten to the ten"—centimeters per second. (This power-of-10 notation is a shorthand way of handling large and small numbers. "3×10^{10}" means 30,000,000,000, or 3 followed by ten zeros. To represent a small number, a notation might be written 3×10^{-10}—read "three times ten to the minus ten"—which is 3 preceded by ten decimal places. It could be written .0000000003.)

How could any particle travel so fast? It was inconceivable—but the facts were there. Belief in the corpuscular theory of light was wavering. But it was far from eliminated as an explanation. Not until almost a hundred years after the death of Newton was the theory proved incorrect. In the early part of the nineteenth century Thomas Young (1773–1829), a prominent physician, teacher, and scientist, performed a simple experiment. He passed a beam of light through a narrow vertical slit. Just beyond the slit was a barrier which had two other narrow slits in it, each at an angle to the first slit. If light was made of particles

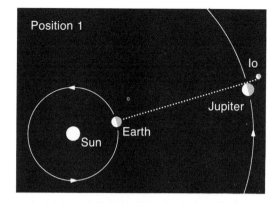

Position 1

Io

Jupiter

Earth

Sun

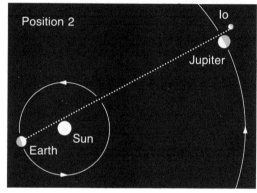

Position 2

Io

Jupiter

Sun

Earth

In 1675 Ole Roemer found that when Earth was at position 1, eclipses of Io (a satellite of Jupiter) occurred at regular intervals of 42.5 hours. As Earth moved, away from Jupiter, toward position 2, the intervals became longer. Roemer concluded correctly that it was because light had to travel farther.

that traveled like bullets, Young reasoned, two bright bars of light, and nothing else, should appear on a screen placed beyond the barrier.

But there were several vertical bars of light—in fact, a series of them, brightest at the center and decreasing in brightness with distance from the center. Young said that light from the first slit traveled in a wave to the slits in the second barrier. Here two waves were created, which passed beyond the barrier to the screen. Where the waves were "in step" there was light thrown on the screen. Where they were "out of step" there was a dark bar.

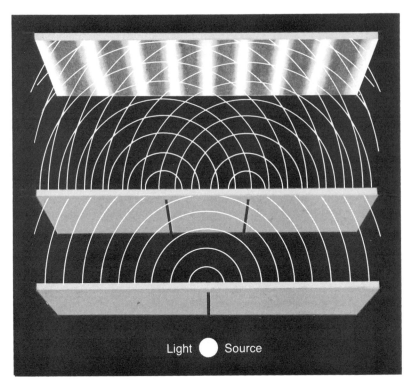

Light ● Source

Around 1800 Thomas Young proved the wave nature of light by passing a beam through a slit, and then through two ad-ditional slits. The light fall-ing on a screen produced both bright and dark bands.

When the light that Young used was one color—yellow, for example—the bright bands were sharp. But when the light was white (which actually is made of many colors), there were fringes of color at the edges of the bands. Young said this was because of variations in the lengths of the waves—and he was able to prove that the red waves are the longest, violet waves the shortest.

Light thus was shown to be a wave phenomenon. The "ether" was still relied upon as the medium through which it traveled.

Much of the behavior of light can be explained by supposing it travels in waves. However, some phenomena cannot be explained in this way. For example, certain light meters work because light falls on a mineral (selenium) used in the meter. The mineral produces a certain amount of electricity for a certain amount of light, and the electricity moves a pointer on the light meter that indicates a measurement of the light falling on the meter. Here light behaves as though it is made of particles. Presently, many researchers refer to light as a "wavicle." When it's convenient to think of it as a wave, that's what they call it; when its behavior resembles that of a particle, then that is the term used.

Scientists often conceive models—of an atom, say, or of the solar system—that enable them to clarify explanations of their observations. The model does not represent literally the actual phenomenon. You might say that the "wavicle" is a model—a convenient version that scientists can manipulate to characterize the nature of light.

Regardless of how we think of light, we know several things about it. We are sure it is energy. It is electromagnetic—as we'll soon show. It radiates into space from a source, needing nothing to carry it. In a vacuum it travels in straight lines at a speed of 3×10^{10} cm/sec.

Light Waves

Light waves radiate in all directions from a source—the Sun, for example. These waves are not like sound waves at all. Sound vibrates in the direction of travel. Molecules of air are alternately pressed together and spread apart as sound travels through them. In light, the vibrations occur at right angles to the direction of travel. And the light wave vibrates in all planes. We show two of them in the bottom illustration on the next page.

Also notice that the high points of a light wave are called crests; the low points are troughs. The distance from crest to

7

crest is called a wavelength. If we measure the number of wavelengths that pass a point in a second—or the number needed to cover a distance of 186,000 miles (3×10^{10} centimeters)—the answer is the number of vibrations (or cycles) per second: the frequency of the light. And, if the wavelength is multiplied by the frequency, the answer is always the speed of light. You could say all this much more simply:

$$\text{Speed of light} = \text{wavelength} \times \text{frequency}$$

Wavelength is the distance from wave crest to wave crest, here shown two-dimensionally. Frequency is the number of wavelengths per second.

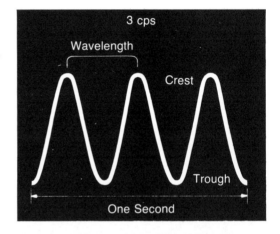

Light is a three-dimensional electromagnetic wave. It vibrates at right angles to the direction of travel.

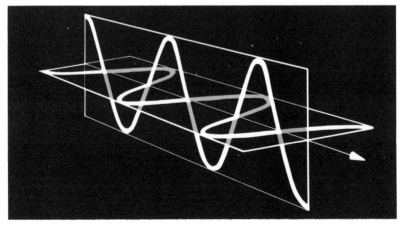

In physics, c represents the speed of light, the Greek letter lambda (λ) is wavelength, and the letter nu (ν) is frequency; so

$$c = \lambda\nu$$

From this relationship, you know that if wavelength goes up, frequency goes down; and if wavelength decreases, frequency increases.

Other forms of energy besides light travel in waves. When the frequency is very high (wavelength short) ultraviolet rays are produced; X rays or gamma rays when the wavelength is only about 10^{-13} meter. When frequency is low (wavelength tens of meters or longer) infrared radiation results, or television and radio signals. When the frequency of the radiation is between about 400 trillion (4×10^{14}) and 800 trillion vibrations a second, light that we can see is produced.

Since the frequency of visible light is high, the wavelength must be very short. It lies between 400 and 700 billionths of a meter. Such numbers are awkward; therefore wavelength is usually expressed in angstroms. An angstrom (A), named after the Swedish scientist Anders J. Ångström, is .00000001 centimeter. That's 10^{-8} centimeter, or 10^{-10} meter. In the metric system, wavelength is measured in nanometers; a nanometer is one billionth (10^{-9}) of a meter. Visible light has a wavelength of between approximately 4000A and 7000A (between 400 and 700 nanometers). (See Figure 1, page 41.)

Colors of light have wavelengths and frequencies as follows:

Color	Wavelength (angstroms)	Wavelength (nanometers)	Frequency (cycles per second)
Red	6500–7000	650–700	400,000,000
Orange	5800–6500	580–650	450,000,000
Yellow	5750–5800	575–580	510,000,000
Green	4900–5750	490–575	500,000,000
Blue	4550–4900	455–490	620,000,000
Indigo	4250–4550	425–455	660,000,000
Violet	4000–4250	400–425	750,000,000

Energy

As we mentioned above, light is energy. It is radiant energy that travels 3×10^{10} cm/sec. It radiates in the form of "packages," or quantities, called photons. (Photons—units of energy—may be used also in describing long-wave radio emissions and short-wave gamma radiation, even though the word "photon" literally means "light particle." The photon was so named because at the time of its discovery its existence as forms of energy other than light was not suspected.)

A photon must be in motion. Otherwise the "package" of energy changes to some other form—to heat, electricity, or whatever.

When photons are of a certain amount of energy, they affect our eyes in such a way that we have the sensation of seeing light. Red light has the lowest energy level—about 1.6 electron volts. (The electron volt is an extremely small unit of energy. One electron volt equals 1.6×10^{-12} ergs. Someone has said that an erg is the energy generated by a mosquito flying full speed ahead. If so, about a trillion mosquitoes would be needed to produce an electron volt.)

As frequency increases, the photon energy increases—up to 2.7 electron volts for violet photons. The energy levels of the various colors are as follows:

Color	Energy (electron volts)
Red	1.6
Orange	1.8
Yellow	2.0
Green	2.2
Blue	2.4
Violet	2.7

Light originates in atoms and molecules that have been excited in some way. To understand how this works, we can consider a model of an atom. You recall that models enable us

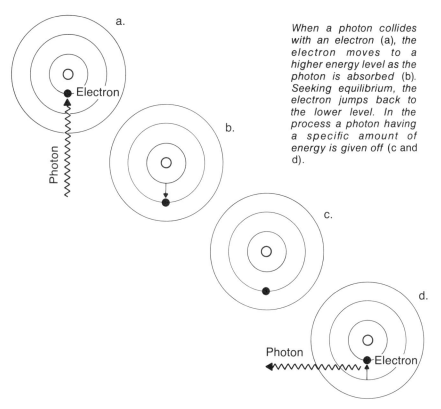

a.

When a photon collides with an electron (a), the electron moves to a higher energy level as the photon is absorbed (b). Seeking equilibrium, the electron jumps back to the lower level. In the process a photon having a specific amount of energy is given off (c and d).

Electron

Photon

b.

c.

d.

Photon

Electron

to see more clearly the structure of something and how it operates. Very simply, an atom is made up of a central core, or nucleus, which contains protons and neutrons. Electrons, located in definite shells, or orbits, revolve around the nucleus. The carbon atom has two electrons in the inner shell and four in the outer shell; oxygen has two electrons in the inner shell and six in the outer shell; and so it goes.

When an atom is exposed to sufficient heat, or when photons possessing a certain amount of energy bombard it, the electrons jump from one shell to another as they absorb energy. The atom has become excited. To become stable (unexcited) the atom must lose energy. The electrons that have shifted to a higher-

11

energy shell throw off photons that move at the speed of light. A certain amount, or quantity, of energy—known as a quantum—is needed to move an electron from one shell to another. When the electron shifts back again, that same amount is set free.

Atoms are often much more complex than the ones mentioned above. For example, in the zinc atom there are thirty electrons arranged in four shells (2-8-18-2), one outside the next. A photon containing a certain amount of energy would be needed to shift an electron from shell one to shell two. To shift an electron from shell two to shell three, another photon of higher energy would be needed. This means that atoms at a certain energy level will give off certain photons; as excitation increases, more energetic photons are absorbed and then set free.

In a gas of low density there is space between atoms—they are not packed together tightly; therefore each atom behaves as though it were by itself. Its electrons absorb certain photons (or become excited by being heated), shift from one shell to another, drop back again after throwing off these photons. The photons thrown off have a frequency depending upon their energy value. This frequency has wavelengths associated with it that may be visible as light of some distinctive color. Atoms of a certain element will always give off the same photons; neon, for example, will always produce the same orange-red color when excited. This is what makes it possible for astronomers to know the temperature of stars, and what the stars are made of—as we'll find out in the next chapter, on the color spectrum.

The Color Spectrum

Before we consider modern understanding of the color spectrum, and how it is used to gain information in the laboratory and out among the stars, we should go back to Isaac Newton. No doubt others before him had seen the color bands produced when sunlight strikes a cut-glass bowl or candlestick or shines through a spray of water; and certainly they had seen a rainbow. But Newton was not content merely to observe. He experimented with the phenomenon and made important discoveries.

Newton cut a narrow slit in a window blind. A glass prism was placed in the sharp beam of sunlight that came into the room. The prism was turned until a band of colors was produced on the opposite wall. The colors were always the same, and always in the same order—red, orange, yellow, green, blue, (indigo), and violet. (Since indigo is hardly discernible, it is often omitted in listing spectral colors.) Newton concluded that sunlight is a composite of many different colors.

To experiment further, Newton placed a red glass filter over the prism so that only one color came through—the red in this case. When this red light was passed through a second prism, only red came through. Apparently, he concluded, red light is in its simplest form; it cannot be broken down into any other colors.

In another experiment Newton placed a second prism so the entire band of colors could pass through it. When he did this, white light was the result. He had taken sunlight apart and put it back together again. (See Figure 2, page 41.)

Newton suspected that the band of colors was produced by different wavelengths of light. But, you recall, his followers did not understand this idea and preached Newton's belief in the corpuscular (particle) theory of light. There was no way of explaining the spectrum by using the particle theory; so the explanation had to come from other ideas, and from other experimenters. Thomas Young, as mentioned earlier, proved that the various colors were due to different wavelengths.

Newton called his band of colors a color spectrum. The word "spectrum" means "image." The band of colors is actually a series of images of the slit through which the light passes. There are so many images that one runs into another and so a person does not see the form of the slit itself. Rather he sees a band of colors in which one color area (made of many images of the slit) blends into another.

When the source of light is a hot liquid, such as molten metal, or solid, such as the filament of a light bulb, or hot gases that are tightly packed together, as the interior of the Sun, the colors produced blend together as in Newton's spectrum. However, if the light comes from hot gases that are not tightly packed together, a spectrum in which the images of the slit are clearly seen is produced. A prism will separate this kind of light into images of various colors, or wavelengths. The color produced by a particular gas—oxygen, for example—at a particular temperature will always be the same.

14

Suppose you were to heat a metal by passing an electric current through it. At first the metal will be red hot. It is absorbing low-energy photons; electrons in the atoms are shifting shells—giving off low-energy photons and dropping back to the original shells. As heat is increased the color changes to orange and then to yellow. Now more energetic photons are involved, and the electrons are shifting to higher-energy shells. If heating is continued, photons of red, orange, yellow, green, blue, and violet are involved all together. The metal becomes white hot. You might try observing this using a clear light bulb and a dimmer switch—the kind often found in a dining room.

Gases behave in the same way. As a gas becomes hotter it gives off wavelengths that are shorter and shorter; it changes color. Therefore, when astronomers know the color of a star, they know the temperature of the star. They know that red stars are relatively cool, their temperature being about 4000° Kelvin. (In the Kelvin temperature scale, the coldest anything can get—absolute zero—is given a value of 0°K. All readings are plus from this point: the freezing temperature of water, for instance, is +273°K, and the boiling temperature +373°K. The three scales in popular use—Fahrenheit, Celsius, and Kelvin—are compared on the next page.)

Betelgeuse is an example of a low-temperature star. The sun, which is a yellow, medium-hot star, has a temperature of 6500°K. Sirius, a very hot, blue-white star, has a surface temperature of about 20 000°K.

Bright-Line Spectra

Newton's experiments with prisms proved that white light is composed of light of various colors. A century later Young's experiments proved that light travels in waves, and that the various colors of light are due to differences in wavelength.

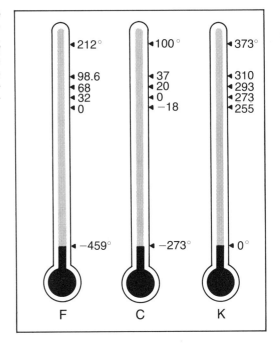

A comparison of three temperature scales—Fahrenheit, Celsius, Kelvin. Celsius will soon be used universally. The Kelvin scale is used in science since it gives a real, or absolute, reading of temperatures.

Newton and Young had succeeded in diffracting light—breaking it down into various wavelengths (colors). Today the "slits" that Young used have become the narrow openings in what is called a diffraction grating.

You can get some idea of what this is by following these directions. Paint a piece of glass, such as a glass cover for a 35-millimeter slide or a microscope slide—or a larger piece if you wish—with black India ink. Brush on the ink to get a thick, even coating. After the ink has dried, lay a metal ruler on the glass and draw a needle along it, pressing hard enough to cut through the ink but not so hard that you scratch the glass. Now draw another line, as close as possible to the first; and continue in this way. If you work carefully, you may get fifty lines in 2.5 cm. (Professional diffraction gratings have thousands of lines per centimeter.)

16

If you've made your grating carefully, you may be able to produce a spectrum with it. To do so, cut a narrow slit, about 2 mm wide (as wide as the lead of a pencil), in a piece of cardboard. The slit should be about 5 cm long. Hold the cardboard at arm's length toward a bright lamp, with the slit vertical. (Under no circumstances ever look at the sun. It is so bright that a glance at it could cause a person to become blinded.) Move your diffraction grating close to your eye, with the lines also vertical. Now look through it at the cardboard. Move the grating and the cardboard to the side until you see an image of the slit rimmed with a spectrum of colors. If the lines on your grating are very close together, the colors will be sharply defined. (You can purchase a diffraction grating from Edmund Scientific Company, Barrington, New Jersey 08007—Catalog Number 40272.)

A diffraction grating or prism is the heart of an instrument called a spectroscope. The observer views light through this instrument. The grating divides the light into its various wavelengths, enabling the viewer to "see" the wavelengths (colors) of which it is made.

Certain elements always produce the same color spectrum. When the substance being studied is heated and changed to a gas, the photons are separated. The spectrum they produce is not a smear of colors; it is a series of sharp lines of color at specific positions. For example, sodium always produces two bright lines in the yellow region of the spectrum. Whenever an observer sees these two lines in his spectroscope, he knows sodium is present.

Colors take on new and additional meaning with the spectroscope. When starlight is passed through a spectroscope, a series of lines, sometimes bright, but more often dark, is produced. (What causes the lines to be bright or dark is explained below.) The series is compared with spectra of known substances. If the lines match, the astronomer knows that a particular substance occurs in the star. We show here the spectra of sodium and neon. (See Figure 3, page 41.) Shown below is the spectrum of a star and the spectrum of iron. Notice that the iron lines are found in the star spectrum. This is positive proof that the star contains iron.

Some stars are invisible. The photons they give off are not energetic enough to produce visible light. The energy is long-wave radiation; it is in the infrared, or radio, region of the spectrum. Other stars cannot be seen because the photons they give off are too energetic to be visible. These are ultraviolet stars and X-ray stars.

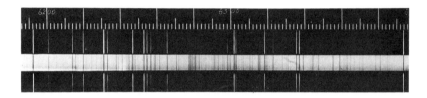

Since some of the dark lines in the solar spectrum (the gray central band) match with the lines produced in a laboratory by gaseous iron (the lines above and below the central band), researchers know that iron exists on the Sun.

The Solar Spectrum

A continuous spectrum, such as that studied by Newton, gives very little information about the light source. There are so many lines, and they are so close together, that the information is smeared. Bright-line spectra are extremely valuable because the lines are discrete and so identify the materials producing them. Except for rare instances, as just preceding a total solar eclipse, the spectrum of the Sun is dark-line. That is, wherever there would be lines of color in a bright-line spectrum, there are dark lines instead. This is why.

Energy from the Sun is produced in the interior, where the gases are packed together tightly. Therefore the spectrum

18

produced there is continuous. (You recall that the bright images of the slit are seen only when atoms are far apart—when the light is produced by gases that are not packed tightly together.) However, as distance from the central part of the Sun increases, the gases become less dense (not as tightly packed). As photons from the center pass through these gases, some of them are absorbed by the atoms. Since they are removed, the light that reaches us in those particular wavelengths is dimmed. It appears in the spectroscope as dark lines.

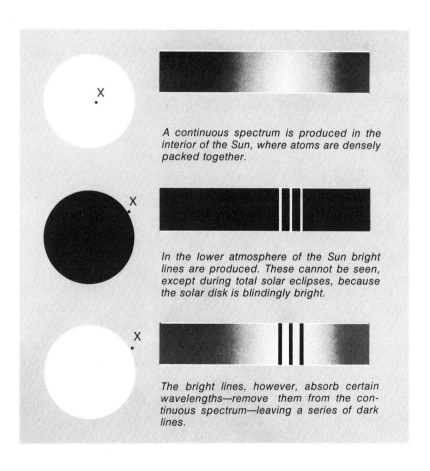

A continuous spectrum is produced in the interior of the Sun, where atoms are densely packed together.

In the lower atmosphere of the Sun bright lines are produced. These cannot be seen, except during total solar eclipses, because the solar disk is blindingly bright.

The bright lines, however, absorb certain wavelengths—remove them from the continuous spectrum—leaving a series of dark lines.

The procedure for identification of substances is the same as for bright-line spectra. The astronomer compares the dark lines with the bright lines of a known substance—iron, let's say—and if the lines match, this is evidence that iron exists in the Sun. Almost seventy different elements have been identified in the Sun in this manner.

Laser Light and Color

Laser light is most unusual, for its spectrum is very narrow, producing only a few sharp, bright lines of color. An ordinary light source, such as a light bulb or candle or the Sun, produces many different wavelengths—a continuous spectrum made of a multitude of bright lines. The waves combine to yield light that is essentially white. It is called incoherent light. In a laser, however, the light is coherent; it is essentially of a single wavelength. The atoms that produce the light are stimulated so that they produce light cooperatively before they can do so independently (incoherently).

The word "laser" is an acronym for *l*ight *a*mplification by *s*timulated *e*mission of *r*adiation. The laser itself may stimulate the atoms in a column of gases, liquids, or solids. A typical one is the ruby laser, which uses a slender ruby column. Ruby contains chromium, among other substances. The laser beam is triggered by exciting the chromium atoms with a flash of intense light. A chromium atom releases a photon—one that is in step with the triggering radiation. This photon strikes another atom, causing it to release another photon of the same frequency. Photons within the column move back and forth. They react with additional atoms, and the number of photons increases until they can be retained no longer. After a few billionths of a second the photons emerge from the laser as an intense beam of light having essentially a single wavelength (color) and possessing high energy.

The energy of the images produced by ordinary light cannot

20

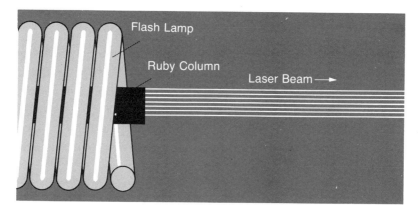

Flash Lamp

Ruby Column

Laser Beam →

In a ruby laser the chromium atoms in the ruby are excited by a charge of electricity, as shown above. In seeking equilibrium the atoms give off photons, which in turn stimulate more atoms.

Unlike ordinary light, laser light is coherent, or organized, as shown below. It can be focused into a beam as tight as a millionth of a meter in diameter—a lot of energy in a very small volume.

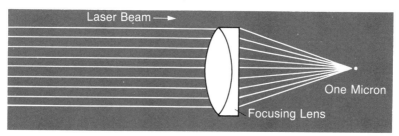

Laser Beam →

One Micron

Focusing Lens

be focused tightly, and so it has to be less than the energy of the light source. However, the energy of the image produced by a laser beam can be much greater than the energy in the column itself. This is because the light can be focused to strike a tiny spot—a micron, which is one millionth of a meter, in size. The spread of the beam is also slight; one 5 cm wide would spread to only 20 cm in traveling 2.5 km. The spread is so small that laser beams have been directed from Earth to Moon-based mirrors, some 380 000 km away, that reflect them back to Earth.

Coherent laser light is a valuable tool that scientists are learning to use in studying the structure of atoms, by bombarding the nuclei. The energy of a laser is also used to drill small holes through steel and diamond. Lasers can set materials on fire in a fraction of a second. So fast is its action that a laser beam can vaporize ink from paper without scorching the paper.

The uses of laser beams will multiply as we learn more about them; we have known about them for only a few years, for they were discovered in 1960. Lasers are of special interest to us because they produce light of one particular color—which makes them quite different from ordinary light producers that yield a wide range of colors.

We have found that color is related to wavelength and energy level; that light which appears to be of one color may be made up of many different colors; and that colors tell us quite a bit about the source that is producing them. But we've said nothing about what is perhaps the most important aspect of all—our ability to see color. How is it that we are able to see and, more to the point, how are we able to differentiate one color from another? We'll try to answer these questions in the next chapter.

The Physiology of Color

The eye collects light and brings it to a focus. The dark area at the center of the eye, the pupil, is an opening through which the light passes. When there is little light, the pupil becomes larger to admit as much light as possible. Should the light be bright, the pupil becomes smaller to decrease the amount that enters. You can see the pupil react to light by watching someone else's eye, or your own in a mirror. First look at the eye under a dim light. Then turn up the light or bring a flashlight near the eye while keeping a close watch on the pupil; you will see it become smaller. Changes in pupil size are especially noticeable in the eyes of a cat. In sunlight the pupil is a narrow slit, while after dark it becomes almost as large as the eye itself.

The eye is made of transparent materials through which light passes. Since the transparent areas are curved, light is bent (refracted) as it passes through them. The cornea is the outer, front part of the eye. Inside the cornea is a liquid called the aqueous humor. "Aqueous" comes from a Latin word meaning watery, and the word "humor" means moisture or liquid. Some focusing of light occurs in the aqueous humor. The main chamber of the eye is filled with a substance called the vitreous humor. It comprises most of the volume of the eye and gives shape to it. It is a gelatinlike transparent substance. The word "vitreous" means glassy.

When light enters the eye it passes through the cornea, where it is bent slightly, and into the aqueous humor. The light passes through the pupil and then through the lens, which focuses the light completely. It then passes through the vitreous humor and falls upon the retina. If light entering the eye were to excite the entire retina, there would be awareness of light but no image would be seen. In order for us to see an object, light must be focused.

The retina is the sensitive inner surface of the eye where light impulses (photons)—some 390 billion a second for red light, 750 billion a second for violet—are received, changed to electric impulses, and fed to the optic nerves, which carry the information to the brain. The light-sensitive optic nerves are connected to rods and cones, two kinds of light receivers named after their shapes. There are perhaps 115 million rods in each eye, and 7 million cones. The cones are distributed sparsely among the rods, except in one region of the eye, called the yellow spot (the macula lutea), where the cones are more numerous. In the fovea, the center of the yellow spot, there are only cones. In this region each single cone has its own optic nerve, meaning there is great sensitivity to light here. In the rest of the eye, eighty cones and rods together may be connected to a single nerve cell.

In bright light muscles partially close the iris (opposite page, top), reducing the amount of light that enters the eye. In dim light the size of the pupil—the opening—is greater.

The anatomy of the eye and the path of light entering it are shown on the opposite page (center). An inverted image is formed on the retina.

Rods and cones in the retina (opposite page, bottom) receive light impulses (photons). Electric pulses generated there are carried to the brain and interpreted as images. Cones are color-sensitive, while the rods are not.

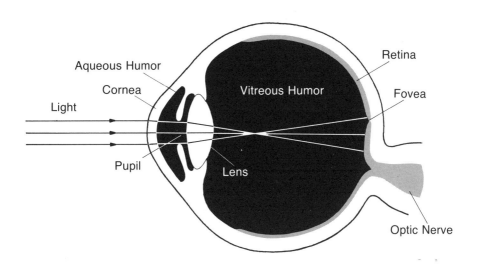

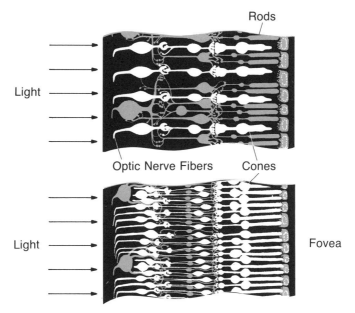

Section of Retina

In the retina, at a region off center toward the nose, there is a small section that contains no rods or cones. This is where the optic nerves enter the eye. Since there are no light receptors here, this location is called the blind spot. You can check for it as follows.

Hold a finger of your right hand about 18 inches in front of you and slightly to the right of your eyes. Looking straight ahead, close your right eye and wiggle your finger up and down (forward and backward); you'll find a position where you can no longer see it. The light from your finger is falling upon the blind spot of your left eye. Switch about and try your left hand with your left eye closed. No blind spot is apparent when both eyes are open because the fields of the two eyes overlap.

The rods and cones are separated from one another by cells in a layer of the retina called the pigment layer because it contains colored matter. The process of seeing involves the change of this deep red pigment, known as the visual purple, or rhodopsin, to a pale yellow substance called retinene. The change is most rapid when the light is very bright. Rhodopsin must be regenerated in order for sight to continue; if it is not, a person loses sharp vision. One especially obvious effect is inability to see well under dim illumination, as at night.

Color Vision

The cones are the receptors that give us color vision. Unlike the rods, cones are not sensitive when the light level is low. Look at a magazine containing color pictures under moonlight, and you'll see the pictures in black and white. The light level is high enough to excite the rods of the retina, but it is not bright enough to affect the cones.

Also, when we see things to the sides of our eyes, we are aware of their presence—and especially so if they are moving— but we cannot discern their color readily. Try this exercise. Looking straight ahead, hold a pencil in your hand at about eye level. Slowly move your arm backward until the pencil is about even with your shoulder. You'll reach a point where you lose the color of the pencil, though you can still see the object. If you jiggle the pencil a bit between your fingers, it will be more visible. At the side of the eye there are no color receptors. Color vision is most sensitive when light falls upon the yellow-spot region of the retina. At the fovea, some two hundred different colors can be distinguished.

How this can be accomplished is a puzzle that has perplexed many scientists. A theory that partially explains color vision, and one that is widely accepted, was developed by Thomas Young—the same Englishman we were discussing earlier—and was later improved upon by Hermann von Helmholtz. Young, as we know, made many contributions to our understanding of vision. Hermann Ludwig Ferdinand von Helmholtz (1821–1894) was a German philosopher, physiologist, and physicist. Like Young, he was interested in all branches of science and made contributions to many of them.

The Young-Helmholtz theory of color vision maintains there are three basic colors: red, green, and blue. In the eye there are three kinds of cone-nerve combinations; each kind is sensitive to one of the three basic colors. When the eye receives red light, the red receptors are stimulated strongly. The green and blue receptors are affected too, but not very much. Should the light be green, the green receptors are stimulated most strongly, the red and blue hardly at all. Similarly, if the light is blue, the blue receptors are most affected. When we see white light, all three receptor types are stimulated equally. The relative sensitivity of the three different kinds of receptors is shown on the next page.

The Young-Helmholtz theory ties in nicely with our current knowledge of color and of the manner in which the range of thousands of tints and shades can be produced by combinations of red, green, and blue—the three basic, or primary, colors, which we'll discuss further in the next chapter. Modern experiments have shown that the process of seeing color is more

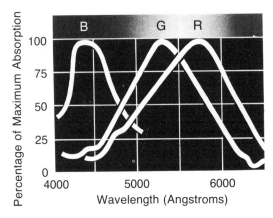

The relative sensitivity of blue, green, and red optical receptors is shown here. Apparently the impulses received by individual cones are not sent individually to the brain. They are first combined in some manner and then transmitted.

complicated than Young and Helmholtz believed. The American scientist Edwin H. Land made two color slides of a scene. A filter that allowed only long wavelengths (the reds) to come through was placed in front of the camera lens when one slide was made. Another filter, one that allowed only short wavelengths (the blues) to pass, was used when the second slide was taken. The two slides were then projected onto a screen through the colored filters. When the two were projected one on top of the other, all colors could be seen—not just red and blue.

Apparently the sensation of a color is related to how much long-wave and how much short-wave light enters the eye. This ratio affects the degree of stimulation of the various cells in the brain responsible for reconstructing the color.

Scientists are far from understanding all aspects of color vision. Certainly they cannot explain fully the workings of the brain—what events occur there and how impulses from the retina are interpreted to produce the phenomenon of seeing.

Color Blindness

When people are completely color-blind, they see everything in shades of gray. To them a colorful scene appears as a black-

and-white movie. However, such a condition is extremely rare.

Suppose you are a trichromat. That's what most people are. It means you are able to see all three basic colors (red, green, and blue) equally well. If you were asked to combine a red and a green light to match a yellow light, you would use about the same percentage of both red and green. If the percentages were quite different from those used by most persons, you would be called an anomalous (abnormal) trichromat—one who sees all three colors, but differently from the way other people see them.

For some people it is hard to separate reds and greens. They appear as either light grays or dark grays—such people can distinguish color intensities but not hues. (Blues can be seen well, however, and also blue-greens and blue-reds.) Red-green color confusion is by far the most common form of color blindness.

The causes of color blindness are not known. However, it would seem that it is due to some abnormal condition of the cones of the retina—the color receivers. In rare cases color blindness may be due to a disease or abnormality affecting the optic nerves. We do know that the condition is inherited, and that it is more common among men than women. About eighty men out of a thousand have some red-green color vision abnormality; but only about four women in a thousand have this defect.

One way of determining if a person is color-blind or is otherwise abnormal in his color perception is by the way he combines lights to match colors. Another way is by what he sees when he looks at color patterns under good illumination. These should not be considered final tests for color blindness, however. The test cards used by optometrists are more reliable as indicators. (See Figures 4 and 5, page 42.)

We mentioned above that the Young-Helmholtz theory assumes there are three kinds of cones in the eye—each kind sensitive to one of the three basic colors red, green, and blue. In the next chapter we shall look at these colors more closely.

Color and Light

Newton's color spectrum was a first step in revealing the complexity of sunlight—light that seems to have no color. And Young's experiments, about a century later, disclosed additional information—in particular about the wavelengths of light.

The prism as used by Newton breaks light into its colors because the speed of light varies from one medium through which it travels to another. The velocity is greatest through a vacuum. When light goes through air, it moves more slowly; and it is much slower when it moves through water or glass. When light passes from one medium to another—from air to glass, for example—the change in velocity causes the light to be bent. If the light enters at a right angle there is no bending; but at any other angle bending occurs, as shown on the opposite page.

If we think of a beam of light as having width, the part of the beam that enters the glass first is bent before the rest of the beam. You might compare the action with a column of eight people marching abreast. The column, which has been walking

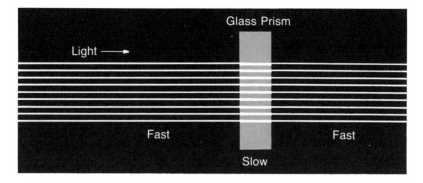

Glass Prism

Light →

Fast   Fast

Slow

The speed of light is affected by the density of the material through which it travels. The light   *entering or leaving a glass prism at a right angle is not bent; at any other angle it is bent.*

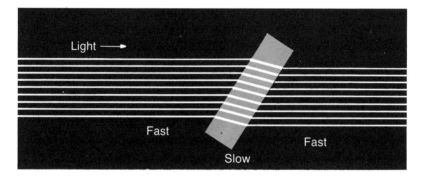

Light →

Fast   Fast

Slow

on smooth pavement, approaches a muddy field at an angle. The first person to step into the mud is slowed down first—the other seven persons move at the same speed. As each enters the mud, his progress is slowed. The effect is to bend the direction of the column. When the column emerges from the mud, just the opposite occurs: bending is in the other direction. So it is with light.

When a mixture of different wavelengths of light moves from air to glass, the longer wavelengths are slowed down (bent) the least. The angle of bending increases as wavelength decreases.

In a prism, such as the ones used by Newton, light is bent on entering and also on leaving. The effect of this double bending is to separate the light into the various wavelengths of which it is made. A spread of colors results—a color spectrum. The bending of light as it passes from one medium to another is called refraction. The control of light by means of lenses, which comprises a large part of the science of optics, is due to their ability to refract light. The separation of light into the various wavelengths of which it is made is called dispersion.

Rainbows

Droplets of water or crystals of ice suspended in the air refract light and disperse it. During summer afternoons, rainbows are seen quite often. Water droplets are held in the air and, for a few fleeting moments, a rainbow arches across the sky. Perhaps you haven't noticed, but the top of the rainbow always appears at the same angle above the horizon. When sunlight strikes those water droplets that make an angle with the horizon of between 40°23' and 42°18', the observer sees a rainbow. Violet will be at the bottom of the band of colors, since it is bent the most, and red at the top.

Each droplet is round. It bends (refracts) the light that enters and then reflects it from the back surface, and you see the light refracted once more as it leaves the droplet. You recall that the different wavelengths are bent at different angles; they then travel slightly different paths and are dispersed—separated from one another.

Maybe you've sometimes seen two rainbows—one above the other. The colors in the second one are dimmer, and they are reversed: red is at the bottom and violet at the top. The second rainbow is not a reflection of the first, as some people believe. It is produced by light traveling a different route through the droplets, the angle of viewing having changed to between 50°34' and 53°56'. (See Figure 6, page 43.)

Sun Dogs—Halos

Around the time of sunrise or sunset you may have seen brightly glowing, many-colored sun images at either side of the Sun, and perhaps an image above the Sun as well. These images are called Sun dogs, or solar halos. Like rainbows, they result from the refraction of sunlight. In a rainbow, the refraction occurs in water droplets; in halos, small ice crystals suspended in the high atmosphere are the refractors. The ice crystals are spread out thinly, so that the sunlight passing through them is bent as though by tiny prisms. On careful inspection you may see that in addition to the solar images, there is an entire circle of light centered upon the Sun. There may also be a smaller circle inside the larger one. However, because of glare, the presence of intervening clouds, or the scattering of light by dust particles, it is rare for a person to see all parts of the pattern at a single viewing.

Ice crystals in the upper atmosphere refract sunlight, producing rings (halos) around the Sun. If one were able to see the entire array of refracted light, it would appear as shown.

Scattering of Light

Rainbows and solar halos, sights we see occasionally in the sky, are caused by the refraction of sunlight and its reflection by droplets of water and crystals of ice. The changing colors of the sky that we see every day are produced not by refraction but by the scattering of basic white sunlight. About eighty years ago Lord John W. S. Rayleigh (1842–1919), an English scientist, first explained the effect, so it is more accurately called Rayleigh scattering.

Gaseous molecules in the air, mostly of nitrogen and oxygen, are very small—about the dimension of a light wave. These small particles scatter the various wavelengths of light unequally. The blues are scattered more widely than the reds. The scattered blue light goes off in all directions. It is reflected to us by dust and water droplets, making the sky away from the Sun appear blue. The closer you look toward the Sun, the whiter the sky seems. This is because you are looking into a region that contains not only blues and violets but also reds and yellows that have not been scattered. For a similar reason, a distant snow-covered mountain appears pinkish. Sunlight falls upon the mountain and is reflected from it. The blues in the reflected white light are scattered; the low-frequency colors—those toward the red end of the spectrum—come through.

You see a red sky most frequently at sunrise or sunset, when the Sun is close to the horizon, because you are able to look closer to the Sun and so see the longer wavelengths. (Remember never to look directly at the Sun.) Also, at these times sunlight is more effectively scattered (blues removed) because the light shines at an angle closer to the surface, and so through considerably more atmosphere, and a greater quantity of dust particles and water droplets—and salt spray, when the view is a seascape. The longer wavelengths can penetrate, however, and they become dominant in the light reaching our sight. The sky takes on a reddish glow, or it may appear quite yellowish. On rare occasions you can see an entire range of colors in the

34

sunset sky, from blues at the zenith to a deep red at the horizon, with yellows and greens between. (See Figure 7, page 43.)

You can see the effects of scattering by experimenting with a glass of milk and a bright flashlight or the beam of light from a slide projector. Focus a spot of light on a glass or a clear square-sided bottle of milk, with a screen on the opposite side. The particles in milk are small and uniform, so selective scattering occurs. From the side, the milk appears bluish. But the color on the screen is pink. The blues are scattered, but the longer wavelengths are transmitted.

Fog Lights

If you've ever driven in a fog, you know that you can see much better when the car lights are turned down. The bright upper beam is scattered by the water particles in the air and is reflected back to you. The light cannot penetrate.

Some cars are equipped with fog lights that enable you to see better. These lights produce an amber or orange beam; the blues are removed by the amber filter. It is long-wave light and so is not scattered as much as white light (containing short-wave blue radiation). The longer the wavelengths produced by a fog light, the better the penetration. Red fog lights (having the longest wavelengths) would be best of all—except that red is not a highly illuminating color. There would be little reflection from objects.

Clouds

Clouds are exceptions to sky color. They may be tinged with color occasionally, as at sunset. But the clouds themselves are gray—from very dark to white.

Clouds are made of layer after layer of water droplets suspended in the air. These droplets are much larger than those particles that cause Rayleigh scattering. All visible wavelengths are scattered equally by them. Therefore you see all the different wavelengths of the sunlight itself—the reflected light is white.

When particles are smaller, the cloud may be somewhat reddish because the shorter wavelengths (the blues) are scattered while the longer wavelengths are unaffected. Clouds appear very dark when the light striking them is absorbed by water droplets and dust particles.

Blue and Green Sea

Scattering of sunlight occurs in water as well as in the atmosphere. While seawater appears to be clear when you look through it from top to bottom, it contains many small particles. These particles scatter the sunlight—the blues being affected more strongly than other wavelengths. The scattered blue light is then reflected to us.

Variations in the degree of scattering in the atmosphere and in the water affect the color that we see. Often seawater appears green rather than blue. This is because light reflecting from the sand beneath (or from light-colored coral) combines with the scattered blue light. The combination produces a variety of blues and greens.

Colors in Oil, Soap Bubbles, and Bird Feathers

Perhaps you've noticed blues, greens, reds, and purples when oil and water are on a tar road, or when there's oil on top of a puddle. There are no pigments or dyes in the oil. Colors appear because of interference in the waves of light that fall upon it.

Light is reflected from the top surface of the oil, and also some of the light penetrates to the bottom surface and is reflected from there. If the thickness of the oil happens to be the same as a wavelength of red light, for instance, red is reflected while other frequencies are not. There is a range of colors in an oil slick because of variations in the thickness of the oil film—the reflected color matching in wavelength the thickness of the slick at that point.

The colors in a soap bubble are produced in the same way. Some of the light that falls on the bubble is reflected from the outer surface. However, some light travels through the thickness of the soap film and is reflected from its inner surface. If the thickness is about equal to a wavelength of blue light—for example—the bubble appears blue; the other colors in the light are not reflected. Because the thickness of the soap film changes, the colors change. You might see reds change to greens and to blues.

The feathers of blackbirds and hummingbirds, the plumage of peacocks, the wing covers of beetles, seem to change color as you look at them from different directions, or as light falls upon them from different directions. They are said to be iridescent. Although they contain no pigments or dyes that would produce a variety of colors, they appear varicolored because light penetrates to various depths from which it is reflected. Certain colors are canceled out while other colors appear.

Green Leaves and Autumn Foliage

The colors that we see in plants are caused by a variety of pigments. In summer, when plants are active, the dominant color is green. This is because of chlorophyl, a green chemical that plants use in the manufacture of sugars and starches. As the chlorophyl is used up it is replaced, so the plant remains green. In addition to chlorophyl, plants also contain pigments called carotenoids. Some of these pigments are yellow; they give color to ears of corn, to lemons, goldenrod, sunflowers. Other carotenoids are much more red than yellow; these are found in beets, tomatoes, roses, carrots. Carotenoids are also present in green leaves. But the green of the chlorophyl is so strong that other colors cannot be seen.

However, changes occur in the fall. No one knows exactly why; perhaps it is because of the cooler nights, the fewer hours of daylight, a decrease in moisture, or combinations of these. The plants stop making chlorophyl and so the green color fades. The carotenoids, becoming visible now, color the leaves brown, yellow, and red. Certain trees (oaks, for example) also produce a substance called tannin as the chlorophyl disappears. This blends with the carotenoids to make brownish yellow, brownish orange, and dull red.

Also in the fall, a group of pigments called anthocyanins form in the outer layers of certain leaves. These pigments, bright red and blue, combine with the others to give leaves the crimson and purple hues we see occasionally.

Notice that the autumn colors are more brilliant at some times than at others. Usually they are at their most bright in years when there has been a dry summer and the autumn air is cool and dry. Apparently that is when anthocyanins are produced most abundantly.

Blue Eyes and Brown Eyes

Look at your eyes in a mirror (you'll probably need a flashlight to get light on them). Around the pupil, the opening at the center, there is a rim of color. This is the iris. The iris opens and closes to adjust the size of the pupil: open when the light is dim, partly closed when the light is bright. Chances are your eyes are some shade of gray—perhaps bluish gray, or greenish or brownish (sometimes called hazel). Or your eyes may be quite brown, or blue.

When a baby is born, its eyes are blue. Actually they do not have any color; the blue is due to scattering of light. The iris is a muscle that is made of fine threads. When white light enters the iris, the muscle threads scatter it. The reds go through, but the scattered blue light is reflected; thus the baby's eyes appear blue. The blue eyes of adults are explained in the same way.

38

As a baby gets older, brown pigment forms on the back part of the iris. If this pigment is dark and heavy, the person has brown eyes; the scattered blue light is not apparent. When the layer of pigment is lighter, the color that results is a mixture of the brown with the scattered blue light. Since the amount of pigment varies from person to person, eye color varies greatly.

The Basic Colors

As mentioned earlier, if you look at the colors in a magazine under moonlight, or under dim illumination inside, you'll see that they disappear largely if not completely. Without light there is no vision; with only dim light there is no color. Most of our light comes from the Sun. It is white light, which is actually a mixture of all colors. We can see some or all of these colors in rainbows, halos, the fringes of clouds, the sea. For the most part, the light of daytime is scattered sunlight, which is somewhat bluer than the light produced by the Sun. When Newton studied light and color, he arranged the colors contained in white sunlight into a color wheel. We find that the whole array of colors can be produced by adding together light in various amounts of three of these colors—the basic colors: red, green, and blue. They are therefore the main, or primary, colors. The color of things—trees, flowers, paintings—results from the light that falls upon them. Change the color of the light, and you change the color of the object. All colors begin with red,

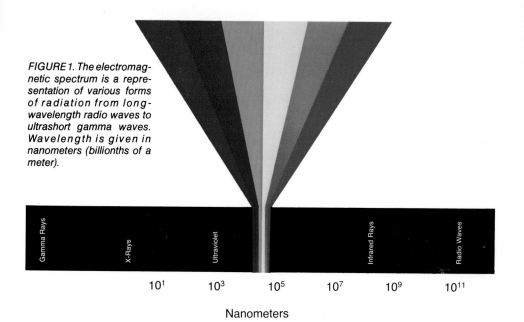

FIGURE 1. The electromagnetic spectrum is a representation of various forms of radiation from long-wavelength radio waves to ultrashort gamma waves. Wavelength is given in nanometers (billionths of a meter).

Gamma Rays

X-Rays

Ultraviolet

Infrared Rays

Radio Waves

10^1 10^3 10^5 10^7 10^9 10^{11}

Nanometers

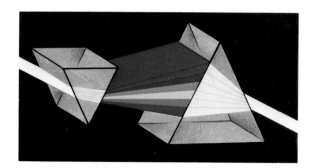

FIGURE 2. Isaac Newton was able to separate white light into the various colors (wavelengths) of which it is composed. Then, by using a second prism, he found he could combine the colors to reproduce white light.

FIGURE 3. Spectra of hot liquids, solids, and compressed gases are composed of so many lines that they blend together to make a continuous band, as in the uppermost example.

Spectra of less dense gases—sodium and neon in our examples here—show bright lines that are separated from one another.

FIGURE 4. An anomalous trichomat is a person whose eyes can receive stimuli from red, green, and blue pigments but not in the usual way. For example, when trying to match a yellow light (center), one such person will select a pinkish light (left). Another trichromat may select a greenish light (right); to him yellow appears greenish and he requires a larger proportion of green for matching.

FIGURE 5. A person who sees all colors equally well would see a color arrangement as shown at the left. A person who can match all observed colors with mixtures of only two primary colors is called a dichromat. He sees the color range as shown at the right.

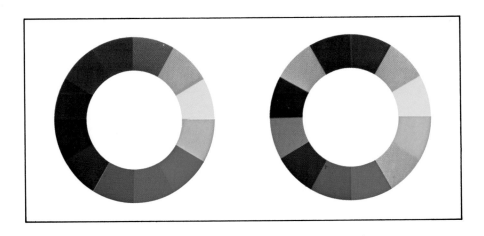

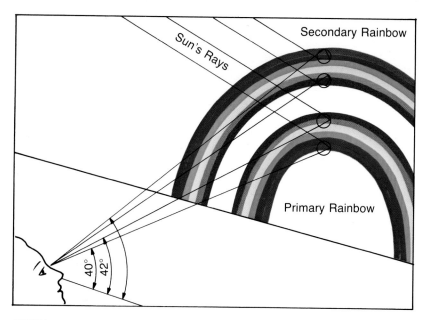

FIGURE 6. A rainbow is produced when sunlight is refracted by water droplets suspended in the air, and is viewed at an angle between 40 and 42 degrees. This is a primary rainbow. The secondary rainbow is seen at a slightly different angle.

FIGURE 7. During the day the sky appears blue because the blue wavelengths are scattered by the atmosphere so that they reach the viewer.

At evening, when the Sun is close to the horizon, the longer wavelengths can be observed and so the sky appears reddish.

Daytime

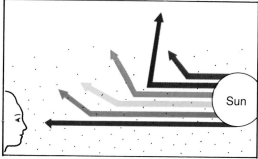

Evening

FIGURE 8. The basic colors of light are red, green, and blue. When mixed together they produce secondary colors and white.

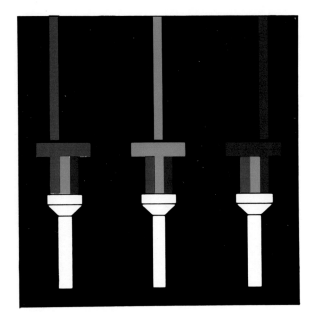

FIGURE 9. Filters remove certain wavelengths (red, green, or blue) from white light.

FIGURE 10. A wide array of colors may be produced by addition. The eye combines dots of various colors, too small to be discerned separately.

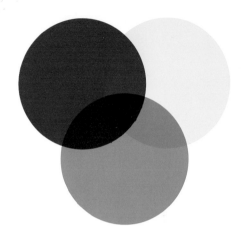

FIGURE 11. In printing, colors may be produced by subtraction. Inks remove certain wavelengths, enabling a multitude of combinations.

FIGURE 12. Some pigments have the ability to absorb certain wavelengths (remove them from white light) and reflect others.

Blue reflected by Pigment

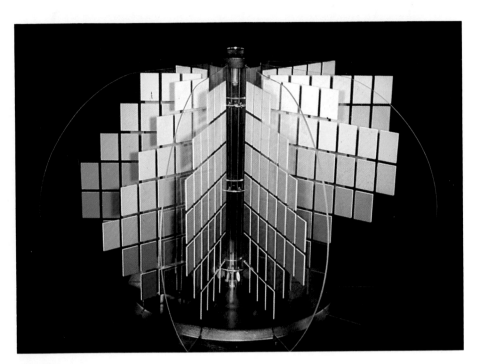

FIGURE 13. The color tree invented by Albert H. Munsell is one way of "measuring" colors. Color chips are identified by three qualities: hue, chroma, and value. The hues are arranged to form the disk of the tree; value is indicated vertically, from black at the bottom to white at the top; and chroma, or color strength, progresses from the center.

POOR VISIBILITY

BETTER VISIBILITY

HIGH VISIBILITY

FIGURE 14. Objects become more visible when there are variations in value.

VIBRATION

FIGURE 15. Highly contrasting colors can be uncomfortable to look at.

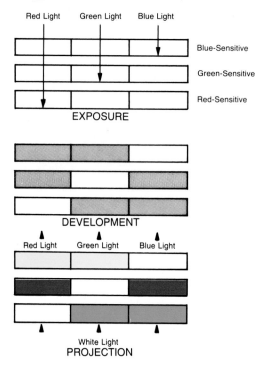

Red Light   Green Light   Blue Light

Blue-Sensitive

Green-Sensitive

Red-Sensitive

EXPOSURE

DEVELOPMENT

Red Light   Green Light   Blue Light

White Light
PROJECTION

FIGURE 16. Color film is made of several layers, each of which removes certain wavelengths (colors) and transmits others.

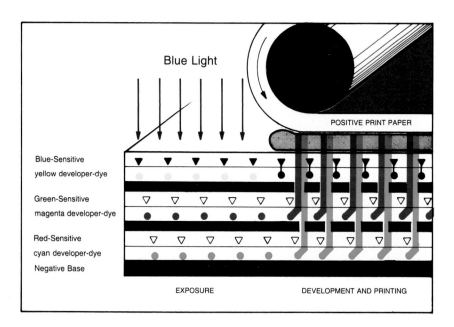

Blue Light

POSITIVE PRINT PAPER

Blue-Sensitive
yellow developer-dye

Green-Sensitive
magenta developer-dye

Red-Sensitive
cyan developer-dye

Negative Base

EXPOSURE   DEVELOPMENT AND PRINTING

FIGURE 17. In quick-developing films the chemicals that remove some wavelengths and transmit others are built into the film-pack itself.

48

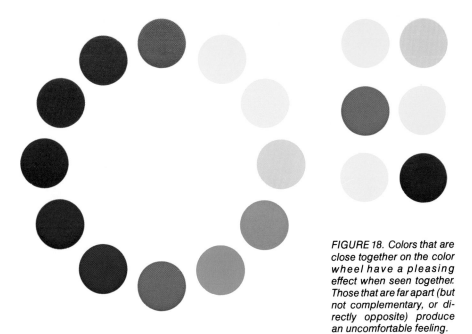

FIGURE 18. Colors that are close together on the color wheel have a pleasing effect when seen together. Those that are far apart (but not complementary, or directly opposite) produce an uncomfortable feeling.

FIGURE 19. Stare at the lower right corner of the star field for about a minute while holding the page under good light. Then slide a blank sheet of white paper over the illustration. Keep staring, and the flag will appear in its correct colors—red, white, and blue.

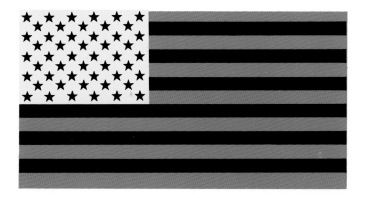

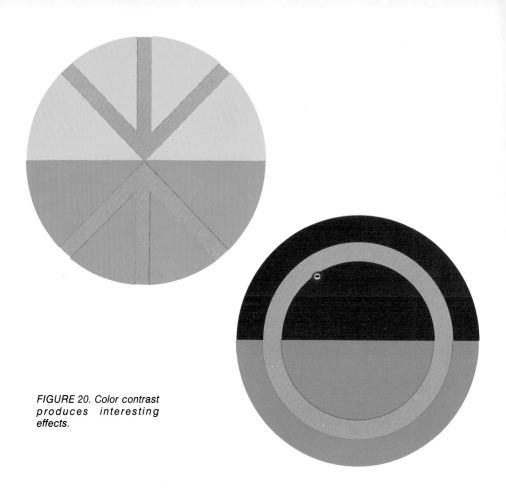

FIGURE 20. Color contrast
produces interesting
effects.

FIGURE 21. The greens in this illustration are the same, although the green on the left appears lighter.

FIGURE 22. Put a pencil across the illustration to separate the left and right parts. Notice a change in the red behind the dots.

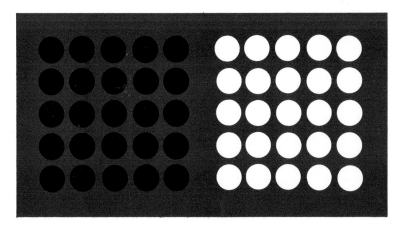

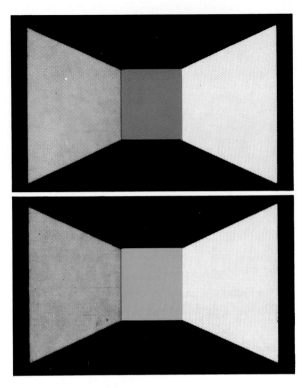

FIGURE 23. The red wall at the end of the hall seems closer than the blue wall.

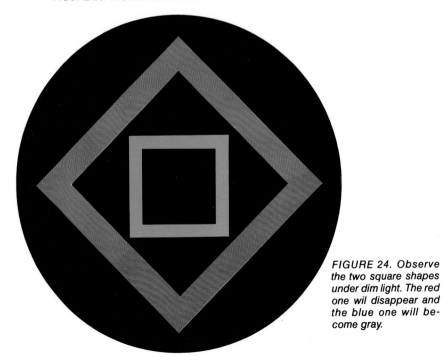

FIGURE 24. Observe the two square shapes under dim light. The red one wil disappear and the blue one will become gray.

green, or blue light, alone or in combination—the primary colors.

You can use the primary colors to produce the color range as follows. Cover the glasses of three flashlights with colored pieces of plastic—one red, one green, and one blue. When the red one is shone on a white wall, a red spot of light is produced. If you shine the green spot so it overlaps the red, yellow is produced. Red and blue together form magenta; and green and blue produce the blue-green color called cyan. White is produced where red, green, and blue light overlap. Actually, because it is difficult to obtain filters having true spectrum colors and also because of differences in intensity among the colors, gray is produced rather than white—generally a slightly pinkish or bluish gray. If you experiment a bit by moving one flashlight closer to the wall or farther away to vary the brightness, more white will result. (See Figure 8, page 44.)

Color by Addition

You can produce a wide selection of colors by the process of adding colors together. For example, suppose you make a spot of yellow light by using a yellow filter. Then add a red spot to it. The resulting color will be a red-yellow—or orange. If blue is added to the red-yellow, white is produced. White also results when red light and cyan (blue-green) are combined. Any two colors that produce white when added together are said to be complementaries.

A filter removes certain wavelengths (colors). So when you use filters over your flashlights you are also subtracting colored light. Let's assume that the flashlight bulb produces white light (all wavelengths of visible light). Now, a red filter placed over the glass removes (subtracts) greens and blues and allows the red to go through; a green filter removes reds and blues; and a blue filter removes reds and greens. (See Figure 9, page 44.)

A yellow filter removes only blue light; red and green pass through. When you shine a yellow spot onto a blue spot you add yellow, which is made of red and green, to blue. Once again you have all the wavelengths, and a white spot is produced.

There are other ways of adding colors together, for example, by seeing two or more colors in rapid succession. The eye holds the first color or colors while the second or third color is added. The brain sees all the colors together—so a single color impression is created.

Cut out several disks of cardboard with diameters of about 10 cm. Color the disks using strong red, green, and blue watercolors. Try various combinations of colors on different disks—one might be half red with the other half painted green; another part red and part blue. Put a pin through the center of each disk and then stick the pin into the end of an eraser of a pencil. To spin

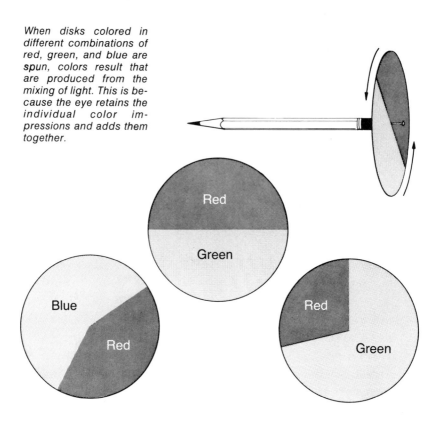

When disks colored in different combinations of red, green, and blue are spun, colors result that are produced from the mixing of light. This is because the eye retains the individual color impressions and adds them together.

the disk, snap the edge with your middle finger. (You can insert the pencil in the chuck of a hand drill.) If the disk is under a bright light the colors will blend together—one color added to another. The two-color disks will produce their complementary colors: red and green will produce yellow, red and blue will produce magenta, and so on. Theoretically, the three colors added together should produce white. However, because of many factors, such as variations in pigments, in the light source, in the speed of the spinning disk, in vision from one person to another, the resulting color is more often a pinkish or bluish gray rather than white.

Color Television

When you watch color television, you are adding colors together. The three basic colors—red, green, and blue—are fusing in your eyes and brain to produce the wide spread of colors seen in the television picture. A color television tube is covered by millions of dots that glow red, green, or blue when they are struck by beams of electrons. The three colors blend in various ways—the viewer observes a color produced by adding one color to another.

Color Printing

Before we discuss color printing, let's take a quick look at printing in black and white. To print a picture in black and white, it is first photographed with a camera that is fitted with a screen, not unlike a fine window screen. The negative that is produced will be made of a series of crisscross lines of dots.

Look carefully at a newspaper photograph. You may be able to see the dot structure. If you use a magnifying glass the dots can be seen readily. The more dots there are in a given space, the finer the picture. Newspapers usually use a screen that gives sixty-five lines of dots to the inch. Quality magazines and books are printed using screens that produce twice as many dots; you may need a very strong magnifier to see them.

You see the colors in this book because of these dots, and because of color addition and subtraction. If you were to look at the patch of color printed on page 45 (Figure 10) through a 7- or 8-power magnifying glass, you would see thousands of red, green, yellow, and blue dots. We also show an enlarged view inside the diamond—the image you would see through such a magnifier. If you place the book upright and move away from it twenty feet or so, the dots will blend together and the enlarged view will take on the color of the outside patch.

Your eye and brain put together the separate dots. As you already know, two colors added together produce a third; and since there are many dots—red, yellow, green and blue—the final color that is printed is produced by addition.

Color by subtraction also plays a part. Printers produce all the colors you see on a printed page by using inks in only three colors. (Black is also used to accent colors and give darker tones to the picture.) The inks are transparent, and so act as filters; they subtract colors. They are not red, green, and blue, the primaries of light that we talked about earlier; rather they are the complementaries of those colors: cyan, which is blue and green; magenta, which is blue and red; and yellow, which is red and green.

In color printing, the paper is run through the press several times, so that one color of ink may be laid over another color. Suppose you were to print pure yellow on white paper. White light (red, green, blue) passes through the yellow ink to the paper, and then passes back through the ink to your eye. Yellow is made of red and green. These two colors pass through the yellow ink, but the blue is subtracted. Therefore you see yellow.

Suppose you wanted to produce green. The printer would print first with cyan (blue-green). This ink passes blue and green. Over this he would print yellow (red-green). The cyan ink passes blue and green but removes red. The yellow passes red and green but removes blue. Since the two inks together remove (subtract) red and blue from the light passing through, only green remains. This ink combination would then be printed through a screen, to produce the dots we discussed earlier. To obtain a greenish yellow, these green dots might be printed alongside red and yellow dots, and a greenish-yellow hue would result.

When all three colors of ink are printed one above another, black is produced. The yellow ink removes *blue*, the cyan ink removes *red*, and the magenta ink removes *green*. Since red, blue, and green are removed, there is no light (color), and the result is black. (See Figure 11, page 45.)

By combining cyan, magenta, and yellow inks, a printer can produce red, blue, and green by subtraction. Now he has six colors to work with. These are printed through screens to combine arrays of different-colored dots. So color printing is a combination of both color by subtraction and color by addition.

Color Pigments

Most of the light that enters our eyes is reflected from an object or a surface. For example, everything in the room where you're sitting is reflecting light. Lamplight or sunlight is falling on the walls, the floor, chairs, tables, and is being reflected to your eyes. The various surfaces and objects display a wide variety of colors. Whether an object is one color or another depends upon the pigment, or dye, that it contains. A pigment is a substance that absorbs (subtracts) certain wavelengths of light and reflects other wavelengths. Pigments are often finely ground chemical compounds, such as titanium dioxide, carbonate of lead, chromium oxide. The compound is mixed with a liquid that holds it in suspension—the particles do not dissolve. Let's see how these pigments produce colors.

Suppose we use a blue paint as an example. When white light

(red, green, blue) falls upon the blue-painted surface, some of the white light is reflected. However, some of it passes beneath the surface, where it strikes small bits of pigment (the pigment for blue might be iron cyanide). The particles absorb red and green wavelengths, and so only blue can escape back to the viewer. (See Figure 12, page 45.)

Suppose, as another example, that the pigment is cadmium yellow, a substance that absorbs those wavelengths that produce blue, but reflects red and green. The resulting color will be yellow. Should a pigment reflect more red than green, the color will be orange.

There are other paints in which the pigment particles are colored but are transparent. When light falls upon such a paint it is filtered through the transparent particles. The light reaches the wall (or whatever surface the paint is on) and is reflected, once more being filtered through the transparent particles. The

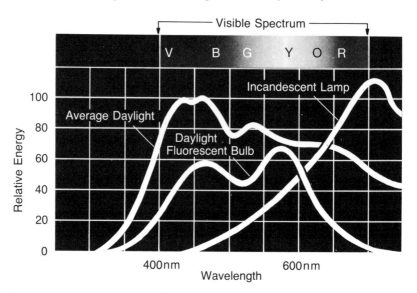

Daylight contains the entire visible spectrum and is strongest in the blue wavelengths. Daylight fluorescent tubes are similar but are strongest in blues and yellows; incandescent bulbs produce mostly red wavelengths.

color that results depends upon the color of the light you start with, the filtering effect of the transparent particles, and the color of the surface from which the light is reflecting.

Another kind of paint, called a lake, works still differently. The lake is made of white particles, each particle covered with a layer of transparent dye. When water is added and light strikes the paint, it is filtered through the transparent dye to the white cores, which reflect it back once more through the dye. By changing the amount of dye, the intensity of the color that is produced can be changed.

Pigments can absorb or reflect only those wavelengths that fall upon them. Sunlight at noontime is white light—it contains red, orange, yellow, green, blue, indigo, and violet. Therefore any of these colors will be produced when sunlight falls upon the corresponding pigment. If the object is seen, however, under electric light (an incandescent bulb), it will appear redder. This is because the spectrum of incandescent light contains relatively more red wavelengths than does sunlight. Under certain fluorescent lamps the object appears more nearly the same as it does under sunlight, because the wavelengths of the fluorescent light are more nearly the same as those of sunlight.

Try looking at color pictures in magazines under different lighting conditions, such as bright sunlight, moonlight, the beam of a flashlight covered with a red filter, a fluorescent lamp. Perhaps you remember shopping for clothes and taking the clothing outside to see the color in daylight. The colors of things change quite a lot when seen under light of different kinds.

Dyes

Many of the objects that you see have color because of dyes. Pigments are composed of substances that do not dissolve— particles that subtract certain colors and reflect others. Dyes, on the other hand, are substances that dissolve completely in a liquid. The particles become extremely small—as small as

59

molecules—and so are not discernible, even under high magnification.

Color is produced in a dye because the liquid itself serves as a filter through which light is passed. A small amount of dye in the solution acts as a single filter; when more dye is used, it is as though the light has to pass through additional filters. With some dyes a thin, or dilute, solution will produce a green-yellow, but when a more concentrated solution is used the green wavelengths are removed and the color becomes red.

The primary colors of light—red, green, and blue—and the basic colors of pigments—magenta, yellow, and cyan—are used in many different ways to produce thousands of different color effects.

Measuring Colors

If someone told you an object was moss-green, or turquoise-blue, or fire-engine-red, you would have some idea of the color. But if you were matching colors to be used in dyeing thousands of yards of cloth or mixing thousands of gallons of paint, such a description wouldn't work at all. One person's description of a certain color is often quite different from another person's. Some way of measuring colors is needed. Over the years several systems have been tried. One that is widely accepted today is the Munsell system, named after Albert H. Munsell, its inventor. (See Figure 13, page 46.)

Hue

We distinguish one color from another—red from green, green from yellow—by its hue. The Munsell system separates colors into ten divisions, or hues. Three of them are the primary colors of light we discussed earlier: red, green, and blue.

If the colors of a rainbow could be spread out and printed on a strip of paper, we would find that one blended into the next. However, there would be five distinctive colors—red, yellow, green, blue, and violet. These become the five basic hues of the Munsell system, except that in place of violet there is purple. Between red and yellow there is yellow-red (orange, as we call it); between yellow and green there is green-yellow; and so on. If the strip of hues is fastened together, we have a disk of ten hues—red, yellow-red, yellow, green-yellow, green, etc. In his system Munsell gave a value of 5 to each of the ten hues; therefore we have 5R, 5YR, 5Y, 5GY, 5G, and so on. The gradations between the ten hues are numbered 1 to 10—so we have 1R, 2R, and so on to 10R. But the hue measurement 5R, for example, covers all reds whether they are light or dark, weak or strong. Obviously additional measurements are needed to describe a color.

Value

Hue tells us what the color is. The value of a color describes how light or dark it is—its degree of whiteness or blackness. If we think of the hues as being on a disk, then values can be represented on a vertical pole mounted at the center of the disk. The bottom of the value pole is black and the top of the pole is white. Complete black is not attainable, so it is given a value of 0; the first step toward white is 1. There are ten steps up to white. Actually pure white is not attainable either, so the highest value a color can have is 9. The middle value of a color therefore is 5.

In the Munsell system, the value of a color is written above a horizontal line—for example, as in $5R\frac{5}{}$. Its hue is pure red, and it is of medium value. If the value number is low (say, $5R\frac{3}{}$) the color will be maroon; if the value number is high (say, $5R\frac{8}{}$) the color will be pink.

Chroma

Hue and value help us in describing a color, but yet more information is needed. Although a pink flower and a brick may have the same hue and the same value, obviously there is still considerable difference in appearance. The difference is one of color strength, or chroma.

Let's go back to the disk of hues and the vertical pole of values. The greatest color strength, or highest chroma, is at the outside of the disk. By even steps, as we move toward the center pole, chroma gets lower and lower until, at the pole, it drops to 0—chroma is gone, and only gray remains.

Chroma is measured in even-numbered steps backward from 16; the lower the number, the lower the chroma. The number is written below the line—$\overline{14}$, $\overline{12}$, and so on.

We now can refer to a color as, for instance, $5R\frac{5}{12}$—a true red having a middle value (5) and a high chroma (12). In just a moment we'll see how these numbers can be used to predict effects.

The range of chroma steps varies for different colors because some colors are stronger than others. Reds, for example, are much stronger than blues; thus red requires more steps to reach gray than does blue.

Also, all colors do not reach the same strength at the same value level. The strongest yellow, for example, is much lighter (higher in value) than the strongest blue. Therefore the complete chroma paths of these two colors will touch the neutral pole at different levels.

Contrast in value increases visibility. If you were to put medium-value red letters on a medium-value green background, the letters would not stand out. However, high-value reds would stand out very well on a low-value red background. (See Figure 14, page 47.)

Bright yellow letters on black or on dark blue stand out very well. That is because you have both high chroma and high value contrasting strongly with low value.

When colors of high chroma are seen together, they contrast so greatly that the effect is uncomfortable. For example, the edges of strong blue letters appear to vibrate back and forth when seen against a strong red background. (See Figure 15, page 47.)

Power

Artists and advertising layout people know that colors vary in their power to attract attention. From the standpoint of the measurement of color, power is a mathematical factor: it is the product of value times chroma. The higher the product, the greater the effect of the color. For example, a bright, strong yellow-red is a powerful color—it has high value and high chroma. In the Munsell system, the color would be $5YR\frac{7}{13}$, giving a power of 91 (7 × 13). The most powerful red turns out to be $5R\frac{4}{14}$, with a power of 56; the most powerful yellow, $5Y\frac{8}{12}$, with a power of 96.

Creating
and Using Color

Before we talk about the way color photographs are made, let's first consider black-and-white pictures. Photographic film is coated with a preparation that contains silver salts. When light reflected from the subject hits the film, these salts change chemically according to the varying intensity of the light. The preparation is washed away when the film is developed. The negative that is produced is relatively darker where more light has hit it, and clearer in those areas that have received less light. To make a print of the negative, light is passed through it onto the print paper. When printed, the photo reproduces light and dark areas as they were in the original subject.

Color Photography

Common color film—the kind used to make transparencies, or slides—consists of three different layers affected by red, green, and blue light, respectively, and a fourth layer that transmits yellow (red-green) light. When you snap a picture, the wavelengths that produce blue are captured by the first layer, or emulsion. Beneath that the yellow layer passes green and red light but blocks the passage of the blue light. Beneath the yellow layer there is a second emulsion, affected only by green light. The red light passes right through to the last layer, where it reacts with the chemicals in that emulsion.

When the film is developed, the yellow layer is removed. Now only three layers are left—red, green, and blue. In each of these, wherever the wavelengths struck the emulsion, silver crystals were removed. The exposed parts are now covered with a dye: cyan dye for the red layer, magenta for the green, and yellow for the blue—the complementaries of the colors in the final print.

If you were to photograph a yellow lemon, on the negative the lemon would be bluish. When the print is made, light shines through the negative onto special paper. The blue dye in the negative passes blue light, which activates a dye in the paper to produce yellow. The original color has therefore been reproduced.

In a color transparency, or slide, there are also three separate dyeing steps. The part of the negative that was sensitive to red light is dyed with cyan, the complementary (opposite) of red; the part that was affected by green light is dyed with magenta, and the part affected by blue light is dyed with yellow.

When the slide is projected, white light from the projector bulb passes through the three layers to reproduce the original colors. Here's how it works, for example, for the reds of the original subject.

The red wavelengths contained in the white light of the projector bulb pass, along with green and blue, through the cyan layer, because those parts of the cyan layer that represent red are clear. In the magenta layer, green is filtered out (magenta passes only red and blue). In the yellow layer, the blue is filtered out—leaving only the red. Follow Figure 16 (page 48) and you can see that the three layers of the film are filters, each removing

66

a particular color from the white light in some areas and passing the light in other areas.

Films are now available that can be developed to produce finished pictures within the camera, or after being pulled out of the camera. The developers and dyes are included within the filmpack itself. Once again the final picture results from subtraction of color.

The film is made up of three layers—the upper one sensitive to blue light, the middle one to green light, and the bottom layer to red light. In each layer there is also a developer-dye combination, producing yellow in the upper layer, magenta in the middle layer, and cyan in the bottom layer.

Let's follow what happens in the case of one color—blue. (See Figure 17, page 48) When a picture is taken, the blue light of the image affects silver crystals in the blue-sensitive layer. The crystals in the other layers are unaffected.

Development begins when a chemical is released that sets the developer-dye molecules in motion. The yellow developer-dye (complement of blue) in the upper layer reacts with the exposed silver crystals, and the molecules are "trapped"—they stop moving. The magenta and cyan developer-dye molecules in the same areas of the other two layers have no exposed crystals to react with, and so they continue to move to the paper in back of the film; there they overlap to reproduce the original blue.

In similar fashion reds and greens are reproduced by the corresponding layers and dyes.

Color Television

A color television picture is produced by millions of tiny dots of color, as mentioned earlier. The dots blend together to create all the variations of color that we observe. A beam of electrons (actually several beams) strikes phosphors in the tube, causing them to glow. The color is determined by the kind of phosphor, and the color's intensity by the number of electrons that bombard the phosphor dot. In ordinary household television each picture is made of 525 lines; that is, the electron beam scans 525 times for each picture. Thirty pictures are produced each second.

The color camera in the studio takes the picture in black-and-white. Inside the camera are color-selective mirrors—mirrors that reflect only red, green, or blue light. These mirrors direct the appropriate beams to tubes in the camera sensitive to red, green, or blue, which generate separate electronic sig-

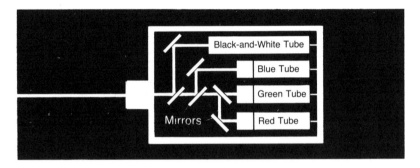

The range of colors on the television screen is produced by combining three color signals picked up by the camera, which are transmitted and received by your antenna and then reproduced on your screen.

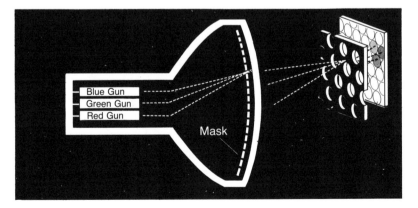

nals for each color. The black-and-white signal is the strongest of all; it provides contrast, detail, and brightness. Weaker signals are sufficient to give good color to the picture.

When your television set is tuned to a station, or channel, circuits in the set separate the signals according to the different colors—black-and-white, red, green, and blue. The signals for red, green, and blue are directed to three electron guns— surfaces that give off electrons when an electric current is introduced—which shoot electrons at the television screen inside the tube. The screen is covered with phosphor dots arranged in groups of three: one for each of the three basic colors, red, green, and blue.

Between the guns and the screen is a mask containing several hundred thousand holes, one hole for each cluster of three dots. The dots and holes are so arranged that the electrons from any one gun can strike only those phosphors that produce its particular color. Variations in the amount of voltage fed into a particular gun will vary the number of electrons and so the intensity of that color.

The color dots are so small and so close together that we cannot see them readily—the separate colors fuse together. Seen through a magnifier, the individual dots can be resolved as being of red, green, or blue.

Colors from Black and White

Disks that have black-and-white patterns on them produce colors when they are spun. This is because the eye varies in the time it requires to register different colors. When such a disk is spun, light of all colors reaches the eye from the white patches. However, the white portions are visible for only an instant at any point, being followed immediately by the black portions. The time is sufficient for the eye to register only a part of the color spectrum contained in the white light, so interesting color effects are produced.

Get several disks of white cardboard (the whiter the better) that are the same size as these circles—8 cm in diameter. Trace the pattern in the first drawing and transfer it to your disk; blacken the area with India ink. Or you can draw the pattern on black paper, cut it out, and glue it to the disk. (Black crayon will not work—it is not black enough and does not cover evenly.)

Put a pin through the center of the disk. Now spin the disk by flicking it with your finger, holding it under a bright light. Or, if you have a hand drill, push the pin into a dowel (or pencil) held in the chuck of the drill.

When the disk spins, it will become a greenish color. Some people see a bit of blue also. Experiment with different speeds and under different lights—bright and dim lights, a fluorescent lamp, sunlight, a strong flashlight, lights of different colors.

This disk was invented in the 1830s by Gustav Fechner, a German physicist who was greatly interested in light and color and their effects. Another physicist who experimented with black-and-white disks was Hermann von Helmholtz, whom we mentioned earlier. One of his disks also is shown here.

If you make your own disk, as explained above, and spin it under a bright light, you will see many different effects, depending upon the speed of rotation, the part of the disk you happen to be observing, and the kind of illumination. The proportion of white observed in a given period of time varies with distance from the center. Therefore different colors will be seen at different locations; for example, you may see a yellow center surrounded by blue, or you may see flashes of orange and green. You may find that as you change your angle of viewing, the color effects will change.

Experiment with the other disks shown here. You might also devise disks of your own design to see if they produce similar effects. When you spin the disks shown below, you'll probably see red circles close to the center and blue circles farther out. Reverse the direction, and you'll have a change of colors.

These disks are fascinating. If at first you don't see the colors, change the angle slightly; or try moving the disk to the side of

Experiment with these disks and with other black-and-white disks of your own design. They produce the interesting effect of seeing various colors—even though the disks contain only black and white.

your field of vision so that it is not in sharp focus. You have to experiment to find how to produce the maximum effect.

Light and Color from Cold Things

In the first chapter we said that light generally comes from atoms that have been heated or otherwise excited, causing electrons to jump from one shell to another. While that is true, there are a few cases where light and color are produced chemically by cold objects, or electrically by relatively cool objects.

When something produces light we say it is luminous, and the process by which the light is created is called luminescence. When chemicals are involved, the process is called chemiluminescence. For instance, when alcohol and formaldehyde are mixed together, the two substances react chemically to produce a glow.

When such a process takes place in a living organism (or one that has been alive), it is called bioluminescence. This is what happens in a firefly. Scientists have found that two chemicals, luciferin and luciferase, in the body of the firefly are responsible for the light it gives off. When these chemicals combine in the presence of oxygen in the air, the yellow-green light we see on a hot summer evening is produced.

When cold-light production is stimulated by electricity, the process is called electroluminescence. A small electric current is sent through a transparent panel. Sandwiched into the panel is a plastic film that glows when stimulated by the electricity. Such panels are used to illuminate meters and gauges that are located in a darkened room, such as a projection booth in a theater, or instrument panels of some cars and airplanes.

Fluorescent Light

Very likely somewhere in your house there is a fluorescent lamp, one that contains a tube rather than a bulb. You'll notice that the tube is opaque—light does not pass through it. That's because the inside is coated with a phosphor.

When you turn on the electricity, ultraviolet radiation is given off inside the tube. (Ultraviolet radiation, often mistakenly called ultraviolet light, is invisible to us. It is radiation that has a wavelength shorter than that of violet light, at the end of the spectrum. It is "beyond" violet and so is called ultraviolet.) When the UV radiation falls on the phosphor, its wavelength is changed to the wavelengths of visible light. Some phosphors produce bluish light; others produce more of the longer wavelengths—those of reddish light. Fluorescent tubes remain relatively cool. The heat that is produced is not needed for light generation.

If you're a rockhound, you know that one of the ways of identifying certain minerals is to expose your specimens to ultraviolet radiation. Some of the minerals that fluoresce are calcite (red), fluorite (violet), and willemite (green). You may also have seen posters, or displays in a museum, that glow in the dark. Ultraviolet sources (sometimes hidden from view) are illuminating them. The minerals, and the pigments used for the posters and displays, contain substances that are fluorescent— they produce visible light when excited by ultraviolet radiation, or by beams of electrons.

When there is a delay in the production of light, the process is called phosphorescence. This phenomenon is used in creating color pictures on a television tube. An electron beam strikes a coating of phosphorescent material, causing it to glow. As the beam moves from one place to another the light persists—and so image motion is smooth and free of flicker.

Light from Excited Gases

The tubes that we see in advertising signs also produce cold light. Color is created when electricity excites a colorless gas inside the tube. Neon gas produces red; xenon produces blue, thallium gives green, and argon shows a light purple.

When electricity goes through the tube, electrons in the excited gas are set free. Occasionally one of these electrons enters an atom, and part of the electron's energy is released in the form of visible light. When the tube is turned off there is no color; the glass is transparent, and so also is the gas inside.

Disappearing Color

As we mentioned earlier, most colors occur because objects absorb (subtract) some wavelengths of white light and reflect others. Part of the light passes below the surface of the object. Internal refraction causes certain of the wavelengths to be retained, and those that reemerge give color to the object.

That part of the light reflected from an object's surface is white—containing all wavelengths. Thus if the reflecting surface area can be increased, the color is lost. For example, when a piece of brilliantly colored glass is crushed to a powder, the color disappears. The powder is white because there are a great number of separate particles, each of which reflects all wavelengths of light. If the powder is wetted with water or clear oil, the color largely returns. This is because the particles now do not act individually; reflection is decreased, and some wavelengths can penetrate into the particles themselves.

You can see a similar effect in the foam made when a glass of soda is shaken (or better yet, a glass of beer). The total surface area is increased because of the great number of small bubbles. Even though the liquid is dark the foam is white, or nearly so. There is a great amount of surface reflection and very little penetration and absorption of the light.

No matter how color is produced—by hot sources or cold, by chemical reaction or electrical stimulation—we react to it in different ways: some colors are cheerful, others are dreary; some colors attract us, others turn us away. Such things have to do with the psychology of color.

74

The Psychology
of Color

Colors have associations that probably are different for each individual. However, certain colors affect all of us in essentially the same manner. For example, decorators consider blue a cool color—a color that would be used in a room having a southern exposure. On the other hand, reds, oranges, yellows, are warm colors; they are used in rooms that face toward the north. Soft warm colors are used in many better restaurants because they make food more palatable; but bright colors are used in fast-food eateries, where the purpose is to keep people moving.

We say a person is green with envy; a beginner is green. If a person is angry, he sees red; when we treat a person well, we roll out the red carpet. Red is a startling, active color. Blue is moody—a person feels blue. We have blue bloods and blue ribbons. If one dons a purple robe, he has become the ruler— purple and royalty go together.

In our society a baby girl is dressed in pink; maybe that's because tests reveal that red is the favorite color of most women. A baby boy, on the other hand, is dressed in blue—

among men blue is the most popular color. A bride is dressed in white; people in mourning wear black. (In China, on the contrary, white is worn at funerals.)

Red is supposed to excite people. Some football teams meet in a red room before the game. To calm them down and provide some rest, the team goes into a blue room during the half-time period.

Things that are black appear to be heavier than the same things when they are green. Tests were made in a factory concerning two crates—one black and one a soft green. A succession of workmen were asked by the foreman to pick up the crates, one at a time, and move them to another location. In almost every case the man picked up the green crate first, thinking it was the lighter one.

When the workman was told to carry the crates to either a red or a blue bench, each 10 meters away, he would almost always take it to the red bench. Bright red is an advancing color; a red object seems closer to you than the same object when painted blue.

Colors make food appetizing. How would you like to eat a gray apple? Or black ice cream? Or a blue banana?

Certain combinations of colors are pleasant, while others seem to clash with one another. The effect produced by a given combination can be determined by arranging colors in a circle and grading them with white and black. The finished product is a circle of hues (the basic colors) with their tints (the color plus white) and shades (the color plus black).

By experience, one finds that combinations of colors that are close together around the circle are pleasing—for example, yellow and green-yellow. If the colors are far apart they are also pleasing—yellow and blue, for instance. But if the two colors are quite far apart on the circle but not far enough to be complementary, they generally produce an uncomfortable effect—yellow and magenta, for example. (See Figure 18, page 49.)

Sometimes, even though opposite colors are used the effect

produced is not as pleasant as might be expected. This is often corrected by altering the proportionate amount of one color. For example, red and cyan (complementaries) produce an uncomfortable feeling when equal areas of the two are seen together. However, if the area of one is much greater than that of the other, the result is comfortable and effective.

Every hour of the day we see colors—the colors of flowers, leaves, birds, animals; the colors in our houses; colors in advertising of all sorts. And we are affected much more strongly by some colors than by others.

In the rest of this chapter we'll take a look at what we might call color curiosities. We'll attempt to explain some of these curiosities through the science of color, but others we'll simply present, since the effects have no apparent explanations.

Afterimages

When you stare at an image and then look at a neutral surface, an afterimage is produced. For example, the flag shown on page 49 (Figure 19) is printed in cyan, black, and yellow—colors that are directly opposite to red, white, and blue. Stare at the lower right star in the star field for at least thirty seconds. (Hold the book under a bright lamp to increase the effect.) Then slide a piece of white paper or cardboard over the flag. Keep staring, and you will see an afterimage of red, white, and blue—the complementary colors of those printed here.

Apparently our eyes have a tendency to generate colors that are complementary to those we are observing. It may be that the retina tires because of the staring. When it relaxes (when you look at the white paper), those cones that were receiving cyan produce red; those that were seeing yellow will produce blue; and those that were seeing black will sense white. Similar effects can be produced starting with other colors—a reddish color will be seen where the original is green, a bluish color where the original is orange, and so on.

Contrast

Both arrows in the illustration on page 50 are the same shade of gray. They appear to be different in lightness—and even in color—because they are on different backgrounds. This is a case of the background color affecting the color in the foreground.

The ring of gray seen in the circle is all the same color and unbroken. Place a pencil along the line that separates the red and blue areas, and you will change the appearance of the gray ring—the upper half will appear lighter, and the lower half will become somewhat pink.

The two green sections shown on page 51 (Figure 21) are printed with the same ink; however, they appear quite different. The reason is that the backgrounds against which the green color is observed are different.

The stripes produce different effects on the same background. Place the book three or four feet from you and take particular notice of the green sections. All the greens in this illustration are exactly the same. The complementary yellow, and the red, cause confusion and lead us to believe the green on the left is much lighter. (You can also see the effect by tilting the book slightly.)

Spreading and Contrast

The phenomenon known as spreading results from a special effect of contrast. Look at the pattern on page 51 (Figure 22), and you will agree that the red color is the same throughout. Now divide the illustration into two halves by placing a pencil between the two sections. The red of one section will appear brighter.

Advancing and Receding Colors

Colors may seem to advance (come closer to you) or to recede (move farther away). The designs in Figure 23 (page 52) are exactly the same, except for the color panels. Yet the red wall at the end of the hall appears to be closer to you than does the blue wall. Designers use this phenomenon to make short hallways appear longer, and long, narrow rooms seem shorter.

Color and Light Variation

When light intensity changes, colors vary. As we mentioned earlier, if you look at the color illustrations in a magazine under moonlight no color will be apparent; there isn't enough illumination. Apparently the rods of the retina are more sensitive to light than the cones—the receptors of color.

You can experience the same effect by using Figure 24 (page 52). Look at these figures in a dimly lighted room; the red object will disappear, while the blue one will lose most of its color. The light must be very dim. In a large room, for example, the only illumination might be a dim flashlight at the end opposite from you. Don't let the flashlight shine on the illustration; just expose it to the ambient (general) illumination.

You are surrounded by color. Notice the colors that are used in advertising signs to attract your attention; the colors in food stores (especially at the meat counter). Different colors do affect us in different ways. Sometimes you may find it hard to explain why you feel as you do; maybe it's because of the colors around you.

And color may account for the manner in which people behave toward you. Color links us to one another—and it does much more. By way of the microscope, light and color guide us into the world of the very small. And via the telescope, they take us into the universe of stars and galaxies. Touch, taste, hearing, and smell provide us with a wealth of impressions about the world. But most of our information is gained by receiving light through our eyes—the sense of sight—and evaluating it in our brains. Color, with its multitude of variations and its many different ways of being generated, is the vital ingredient of light.

Further Readings

Adler, Irving. *Color in Your Life.* New York: The John Day Company, Inc., 1962.

Hagen, Catherine. *Color.* New York: Henry Z. Walck, Inc., 1976.

Hellman, Hal. *The Art and Science of Color.* New York: McGraw-Hill Book Company, 1967.

Neal, Charles D. *Exploring Light and Color.* Chicago: Children's Press, 1964.

Index

vision (color), 26-29, 42, 77
visual purple (of eye), 26
vitreous humor, 24

wavelengths, light (*see also* color; light)
  in color processing, 44, 45, 48, 53-54, 57-60, 66
  definition of, 8
  dispersion of, 30-39
  in fluorescent lighting, 73
  and frequency, 9, 10, 12
  of laser light, 20-22
  measurement of, 8-9, 41
  radiation of, 7-12
  refraction of, 30-32, 43, 74
  scattering of, 34-35
  theories of color and, 5-6, 14-15, 27-28, 30
wave theory of light, 2-3, 5-7, 14

"wavicles," 7
white, 53-55, 62, 76, 77
white light, 6, 14, 15, 20, 27, 36, 40, 41, 44, 59, 69, 74
  scattering of, 34-35, 36, 38-39, 40, 43

xenon, 73-74
X rays, 9, 18

yellow, 13, 77
  in color printing, 56-57
  measurement of, 61, 63
  processing of, 53-55, 66-67
  psychological effects of, 75, 76
  in scattered light, 34
  wavelength of, 9
yellow spot (of eye), 24, 27
Young, Thomas, 4-6, 14, 27-28
Young-Helmholtz theory, 27, 29

About the Author

Franklyn M. Branley, Astronomer Emeritus and former Chairman of The American Museum–Hayden Planetarium, is well known as the author of many books about astronomy and other sciences for young people of all ages. He is also coeditor of the Let's-Read-and-Find-Out Science Books.

Dr. Branley holds degrees from New York University, Columbia University, and the State University of New York College at New Paltz. He and his wife live in Woodcliff Lake, New Jersey.

About the Illustrator

Henry Roth is a photographer-painter. He has produced television commercials, and he both produced and directed an educational film and a film for New York's Joffrey Ballet. His meticulous illustrations have appeared in several science books, among them Franklyn Branley's Energy for the 21st Century.

Mr. Roth was born in Cleveland, Ohio, and received his degree from the Cleveland Institute of Art. He now lives in New York City.